# Identity Theft

*Are You Protected From The Thief?*

By

Dr. Ric Perez

# Identity Theft
*Are You Protected From The Thief?*

By

**Dr. Ric Perez**

Copyright @ 2018, All Rights Reserved
Printed in The United States of America

Published By:

**ABM Publications**
A division of HSBN Publishing
PO Box 6811, Orange, CA 92863

ISBN: 978-1-931820-86-8

All scripture quotations, unless otherwise indicated are taken from the King James Version of the Bible, Public Domain. Those marked AMP are from the Amplified Bible, copyright @ 1987, The Updated Edition, by the Zondervan Corporation and the Lockman Foundation, and is used by permission. All rights reserved.

## DEDICATION

To my loving wife & partner in life,

*Maria*

## TABLE OF CONTENTS

|   | INTRODUCTION | 7 |
|---|---|---|
| 1 | A SEASON of CHANGE | 9 |
| 2 | DIVINE IDENTITY excludes CORRUPTION | 17 |
| 3 | DIVINE IDENTITY is at RISK | 21 |
| 4 | IDENTITY can be STOLEN | 25 |
| 5 | IDENTITY is NEW | 37 |
| 6 | 5 EQUIPPINGS TO PROTECT and GUARD YOUR IDENTITY | 47 |
| 7 | DEVOTIONS - Prophetic Words of Divine Encouragement | 59 |
|   | ABOUT THE AUTHOR | 65 |

## INTRODUCTION

Let's start this journey with the absolute Truth, with no frill or fuss. Plain and simply put you are in possession of an extremely valuable and priceless asset. What you hold is unique and cannot be duplicated. It is rare and abundant only in you. There are no secret reserves of this asset, nowhere in all of creation can this be located. Yes, it can only be found in you. It is your *Identity*!

The dictionary defines *Identity* as "the fact of being who or what a person or thing is...". The main characteristic is an association with an outside resource, this in turn can assist in the determination of ownership or direction. But when ownership is present sometimes the world see's what you have and so it sets its eyes with envy and begins to author plans to take what does not belong to it. We have all read or heard of accounts from thieves, once caught, they reveal their tools of the trade, as it were, casing out a target to steal from the owner, a rare a priceless jewel or piece of art.

The spiritual world is no different. There is a plan to delay, hinder and even cancel what God has set into motion. Our rejection of such activity or plan only places the individual at great risk and even peril. There is a perfect plan authored by God and this plan includes you. Your success in this plan is founded upon your awareness of your *Identity*.

In the pages that follow, you will learn to not only see the value, but you will also learn what can be done to protect this valuable asset called your *Identity*. If you do not understand it then the many that will come to destroy it will be successful and this is what this Holy Spirit teaching has come to prevent. If you do not take measures to provide some type of security or strong perimeter to protect it then a thief will come to steal it.

Walk with me in this Holy Spirit led teaching and journey which has been designed for your full edification, leading to your complete equipping. It is best stated in Jeremiah 29:11

*"For I know the thoughts that I think toward you,*

*says the Lord, thoughts of peace and not of evil,*

*to give you a future and a hope."*

Chapter 1

## **A SEASON of CHANGE**

A Season of Change is now upon you, not necessarily evident nor understood, nevertheless a change was now in full motion. In Galatians 2:20 (NKJV) we read

*"I have been crucified with Christ; it is no longer I*
*who live, but Christ lives in me;*
*and the life which I now live in the flesh*
*I live by faith in the Son of God,*
*who loved me and gave Himself for me."*

In these words you are reminded that something has happened. You started something as your old self, but a transformation is now in process. You are becoming less and less like you. In fact a time will arrive when you will no longer be recognizable to yourself.

But now I want us to look at the same verse but through the translation of the Amplified Bible. It reads

*"I have been crucified with Christ;*
*(that is, in Him I have shared His crucifixion)*
*it is no longer I who live, but Christ lives in me;*
*and the life which I now live in the flesh I live by faith*

*(by adhering to, relying on, and completely trusting) in the Son of God, who loved me and gave Himself for me."*

The time for change comes in many shapes and forms. Sometimes we know when this season is upon us while other times we would prefer to ignore it and continue as in previous times.

Let's take a look at Acts 9:3-6. The Word of God describes a Season of Change the best way to understand it:

*"As he traveled he approached Damascus, and suddenly a light from heaven flashed around him and he fell to the ground and heard a voice saying to him, "Saul, Saul, why are you persecuting and oppressing Me?" And Saul said, "Who are You, Lord?" ….."*

God had a plan for Saul of Tarsus. This plan would not only change him into Paul but it would change the world forever. This plan demanded a change not only to his thinking and spirituality but it would demand a change to his *Identity*. The very things he previously found as important truths in his life would be ripped from his possession and in their place God would hand him new perspectives. Paul would be forever changed and because of this he would lead others in their journey.

In this new season of change, you might even consider calling it a "season of discarding". In other words it is a time to start over by discarding what cannot be used. When the old is discarded, the new can be built. Your new Identity cannot be built upon the weakened foundation of what once was, it requires a fresh vision and a new understanding.

The first of 3 areas I want you to focus your discarding skills upon is your "former nature". Your new *Identity* is precious and priceless and cannot use your former methods, traditions and attitudes. These no longer serve any value and Ephesians 4:22-24 in the Amplified Bible confirms this as follows:

*".... [completely discard your former nature],*
*which is being corrupted through deceitful desires,*
*and be continually renewed in the spirit of your*
*mind[having a fresh, untarnished mental and spiritual*
*attitude], and put on the new self*
*[the regenerated and renewed nature],*
*created in God's image, [godlike]*
*in the righteousness and holiness of the truth*
*[living in a way that expresses to God*
*your gratitude for your salvation].....*

The second of 3 areas I want you to focus your discarding skills upon are your "former expectations".

What exactly are these expectations? Simply put these are those ideas, hopes and desires that we focus upon. These can include old dreams and goals that have not come to pass. They can include people and objects and can even get to the point of idolatry.

Sometimes we focus our expectations on these so much that we no longer hear the directions of God nor are we able to see God doing anything new in our lives. In this season your Identity must be protected at any cost. Do become lost in expectations that do not have God in the front. Remember the words of Isaiah 43:19...

*"Do not remember the former things, or ponder the things of the past. "Listen carefully, I am about to do a new thing, now it will spring forth; Will you not be aware of it? I will even put a road in the wilderness, Rivers in the desert."*

The third area I want you to focus your discarding skills upon is your "former habits". These can include the way we pray, meditate, worship and even minister to each other. As your new Identity is being established through your strengthened relationship with God, these former habits, some bordering on the fanatic and cultish, have no value and power any longer. It is this former habit which much be discarded as quickly as possible. It is here where judgment is birthed, nurtured and harbored. Deuteronomy

2:1-3 states that habits must be broken before you can travel into a new direction:

> *"Then we turned and set out for the wilderness by the way of the Red Sea, just as the Lord had told me; and we circled Mount Seir for many days. And the Lord spoke to me, saying, 'You have circled this mountain long enough; turn northward..."*

Now with some added understanding from the Hebrew and Greek perspectives we see that we too are involved at the Cross. Your *Identity* can be found at the foot of the Cross and in no other place.

You can try all types of remedies, money, love, sex, drugs, the list is endless but none of these will ever reveal your true *Identity*. You will only remain the same, but as soon as you understand that Jesus made a way for your true Kingdom *Identity* to be released and for you to operate in your full giftings, then everything changes. As we read further we see that there was a time that we lived by the flesh or in the world. This can include rebellion against the Call of God to the self-righteous positions of idolatry. But when you are truly on the road to the discovery of your *Identity* in Christ, you begin to realize that it is not about you and completely about the Son of God.

This new perspective reveals the importance of the development of your faith. Not just a religious or traditional development of faith, but one that is truly born of the Kingdom of God. The type of faith our spirit desires but which has never been located. In the Amplified translation we read the definitive components of true faith. It is these components that religion does not teach you nor does it reinforce them because religion has not concerned itself with the development of these critical keys in your life. Romans 10:11describes faith as *"...adhering to, relying on, and completely trusting..."*. Faith is serious business; your spiritual *Identity* is based on these important keys. Hebrews 11:6 teaches us

*"But without faith it is impossible to please Him,*

*for he who comes to God must believe that He is,*

*and that He is a rewarder of those*

*who diligently seek Him."*

The development of our faith is essential if not critical to the complete understanding of who you are in Christ. This requires you to do the following: adhere, rely and trust to a brand-new level, a new plateau. The constructs of religion have developed a people that only trust on what can be seen. Proverbs 3:5 sets the stage for our proper direction:

*"Trust in the Lord with all your heart, and lean not on your own understanding..."*

Our success in the development of trust is not to be founded upon our flesh, feelings or emotions. These will always prove to be incorrect and will mislead us. When the existence of faith is dependent on the presence of proof that is not faith. The body of Christ has been polluted with this enemy. It is now time for the Body of Christ to rise up in power and understanding. No more rituals which rob us of wisdom. No more new age references which only cause chaos and confusion. Army of God arise!

The true opposer is the liar that waters down the need for the understanding of who one is in Christ. Your *Identity* is at risk every moment, yet God has provided a way for you to follow so that rather than be at risk, you would be transformed and empowered to become the victor rather than the defeated.

## PERSPECTIVES

1. **If you lose your *Identity*…. then you lose your momentum**

*When you do not stay in the presence of the Word of God this is the equivalent to leaving your front and back doors to your home opened. This will surely invite the thief who will take what does not belong to it. This event will bring chaos and will halt your spiritual forward progression.*

2. **If you lose your *Identity*... then you will be moved by the world and not by God**

   *When the Word of God is absent in our lives we will soon find ourselves being moved and motivated with desires of the world. Soon our movement will no longer be Kingdom focused rather it will be that of the flesh.*

3. **If you lose your Identity...you will forget who you are and following the Will of God will be impossible.**

   *When you can no longer connect your Identity with Divine origin or purpose, completing or continuing the Plan of God for your life becomes impossible.*

Chapter 2

## DIVINE IDENTITY excludes CORRUPTION

Your *Identity* is Jesus, that place of peace and understanding that you will find yourself resting within, it is an amazing and powerful place to reside. Not only is it a place with peace as a standard resource but it is a revelation filled environment.

Whatever your need happens to be, it is a place whereby all hidden and secret things would be revealed to you. Why? Because as long as you are walking upon the path as appointed for you by God, He will ensure the clarity of His vision and resources be sufficient for you. Victory is ordained, and loss is to be foreign!

Yes, there was a time when we were divorced from all of His bountiful appointments. A power Truth can be found in Ephesians 4:22

*"...that you put off, concerning your*
*FORMER conduct the old man*
*which grows CORRUPT according to the deceitful lusts,*
*and be renewed in the spirit of your mind,*
*and that you put on the new man*
*which was created according to God,*
*in true righteousness and holiness."*

When we walked alone in a selfish state, or as this verse describes as *"former conduct"*, defined as that walk that we did not want to follow or that life that we did not want to live. But thanks be to God that it was a "former" state or condition. So, if you have accepted Jesus into your life, then you are now being reconnected to your *Identity*.

Your mind and spirit are now in the process of being renewed. Psalm 51:10

*"Create in me a clean heart, O God, and renew a steadfast spirit within me..."*

As these are renewed, as your heart starts to become softened by the Presence of Jesus in your life, you will day by day start to keenly understand who you are and how precious your *Identity* is to Him. Remember there was a great and rare price paid for you. It was so unusual and complete that nothing like this would ever come again. So precious was His sacrifice that no price tag will ever correctly display its cost. Even the word priceless seems to inadequately describe its value!

There is something happening within you once your old way of thinking and religiosity is replaced by His newness! You will begin to start the rejection process of the world and you will begin to filter out and restrict what once was acceptable in your life. Your spiritual *Identity* is being formed. True righteousness and holiness will become increasingly more important to you than "fitting in" or in "being accepted". Romans 8:28 instructs us:

*"And we know that all things work together for good to those who love God, to those who are the called according to His purpose."*

This is only possible because the revealing work of the Holy Spirit is at hand. From here no longer will corruption, deception and lust be your desire. You are changing position, there is a shift in progress. Your *Identity* is being revealed to you!

## PERSPECTIVES

### 1. Always know where you are standing

*It is always necessary to know the path and direction you are traveling. When you take your eyes off of the road you will end up traveling to a place not intended, a foreign land. Through the revelation of the Holy Spirit, through an ever increasing and strengthened relationship with Jesus, you will always know where you stand. You will always know who you are!*

### 2. Stop focusing on your previous self

*Your former self, the person you used to be prior to you committing to a life of Christ, no longer is necessary. That person now, is in an ever-changing mode. He or she is now directed toward a new life with a new purpose and goal. When you focus on what is ahead rather than what is behind, victory and success will always be your friend.*

### 3. Renewal is critical to your growth

*Everything about your relationship with Christ is intended to renew you both spiritually and naturally. Through this new understanding of your Kingdom Identity, the thief can no longer hijack your thinking or progress. Change is not always welcomed nor comfortable, but when the Spirit of God delivers change through revelation, the end result is your growth and even promotion. Renewal is the catalyst to new seasons and successes.*

Chapter 3

# DIVINE IDENTITY is at RISK

It seems that any time something good is placed out there in the open, there is always someone or something ready to take it away. The Word of God instructs us that we live in a fallen world. Ephesians 6:12 instructs us

*"For we do not wrestle against flesh and blood, but against principalities, against powers, against the rulers of the darkness of this age, against spiritual hosts of wickedness in the heavenly places."*

The very things that have surrounded us are the very things that are of the world, like spiritual vultures if you will, making plans to take what is divinely in your possession. To put this in an even more personal perspective, there is an enemy that encircles those who love God. We must come to understand that our God is our shield and it was He, through the Blood of Jesus, that made it possible to be protected at all times.

Here is the warning. Do not let yourself become consumed with the "enemy" or "spiritual warfare" perspective. When you are secure in who your *Identity* is founded upon and when your understanding has become solidified in Kingdom wisdom, you will live a life that is promoted by the Kingdom of God and not demoted nor delayed with the things of the enemy. Yes, there is a spirit in this world. Yes, there is darkness, but let us place more time and attention to the plans of God and His presence in our lives.

The Bible is very clear about the adversary and its designs. Thieves do not come to steal objects of no value. In other words, the diamond thief steals diamonds not because of their compounds but because of their worldly value. The rare art thief does not steal rare paintings because of their beauty but because of the monetary value they command in the black market. The same is true in the spiritual. The thief I speak of is the one referenced in John 10:10 (AMP)

*"The thief does not come except to steal,*

*and to kill, and to destroy...".*

This thief comes to steal your *Identity* by stealing your level or measure of faith. It comes to destroy what God has built up within you. This thief comes not only to steal, to take what does not belong to it, but it comes to kill and to destroy the very presence of it in your life. A life without faith is a life without realizing ones true *Identity* in Christ.

If this enemy can steal and even remove from your presence, through destruction, the very seeds of victory and success that stem from your divine perspective found in your true *Identity*, then it will use everything at its discretion. This verse continues:

*"... I have come that they may have life, and that they may have it more abundantly (to the full, till it overflows.)"*

Jesus gives you a guarantee, one not to be taken from a religious perspective but from a victorious and eternal position. There are pressures both natural and spiritual that we will encounter on a regular basis. Some we will pass while others we will struggle with, but the guarantee is that if we included Jesus' positions for me in my life, I am destined to have more than what my understanding can handle.

Another perspective for you is your *Identity*. If you first understand yourself better in the spiritual position, then your success and victory in the natural environments will follow suit as all good things come from our Father. Your *Identity* is a powerful tool to wage war against every enemy, against every adversary known to man. When you stand firmly upon the promises of God for your life you will see new growth spiritually and then the manifestations of victory begin.

# PERSPECTIVES

### 1. Do not hand over your Identity to the liar

*You are to be in possession at all times. The world will attempt to use such ploys as failure and condemnation to separate you from the understanding that you are a child of the most High God. Always remember the enemy is a liar and will uses every trick know to humanity to divide you from your spiritual Identity.*

### 2. The liar steals understanding of purpose

*The opposer will come into your life, usually when you are separated from the Word of God or through some type of heaviness or season of extreme weariness. It will bring cloudiness of purpose. Its goal is to make revelation and understanding unattainable.*

### 3. The liar kills your desire to move forward

*When your Identity has been compromised your future appears bleak. It soon becomes very difficult to continue moving forward with any hope or optimism. The thief has stolen the most valuable of assets and not your desire has suffered.*

Chapter 4

## IDENTITY can be STOLEN

Let's make it very clear, your *Identity* is extremely valuable and there is definitely a thief prowling and lurking in your camp making plans for its theft. The world offers many alternatives and areas to hijack your focus from your purpose so that you would not pursue the things of the Kingdom. Matthew 6:19 tells us

> *"Do not lay up for yourselves treasures on earth, where moth and rust destroy..."*

One of the many diversions it will employ will be to have you get so focused on the things of the world that it now becomes an idol. Many want to do the Will of God but get consumed and even side tracked by their desires, careers and problems. They say one thing but end up doing another. This has become a common occurrence in the life of a believer.

In these days of technology and social media, it is very easy to get over involved in the things not of God. If we are going to protect what God has given us, then we are going to have to redirect our thinking and especially our perspective. Do not focus on worldly goals but on the goals and plans of the Kingdom of God. Everything of the world will rot and rust, it has no sustainability. There is no value in comparison to divine plans. But when your *Identity* has yet to be revealed, or until you understand just how precious you are in the eyes of our heavenly Father, your focus is diverted from the real purpose. You must be on alert at all times! The complete verse reads

*"Do not lay up for yourselves treasures on earth, where moth and rust destroy and where thieves break in and steal...".*

In the world, a place that rejects God and His plans is a place whereby thieves enter by force and take what has a divine value. The only protection you have is the Word of God. The only weapon you can wield against an invisible thief is the Word of God. The only security system available to you is the Word of God.

When our understanding is correct because our *Identity* is in order, then we will most definitely understand that God has a plan for our lives. It is when I am not in His presence daily, it is at this point that the thief enters, and my understanding suffers. In this place faith is weakened and when I need it the most it is not present or insufficient to support me. Never forget Jeremiah 29:11

*"For I know the thoughts that I think toward you, says the Lord, thoughts of peace and not of evil, to give you a future and a hope."*

God has a specific plan for your life and it requires your *Identity* to be founded and set in His Truth and not in the lies of the world. The plan of God for you is amazing and is filled with peace and hope and is completely void of evil. So, when evil strikes, or when chaos or confusion manifest, rather than blame God for His lack of aid, I must assess my position. Have I drifted? Have I excluded Him in my life yet expecting Him to manifest when I need Him? If you answered "yes" to any of these questions do not worry and most definitely do not give up because God has not given up on you.

His plan for you is never removed and His plan for you remains great. Just get back into the relationship. Grab your bible and restart your spiritual relationship with Him. This is exactly what the enemy does not want you to do. But if you do then you will find yourself right back where you left off and even in a stronger position.

Your destiny has a divine authorship and purpose. Psalm 37:23 tells us:

*The steps of a good man are ordered by the Lord...*

When your heart desires Kingdom focus then you must know that every step you take has a divine purpose. When you walk in Christ you are *"in order"*. But when we do not, when we make choices that are contrary to this purpose, then we are *"out of order"*. The target here is to remain in the position described above as *"a good man"*. In the world that carries a different understanding than what God is describing and expecting. A biblical "good man" is someone who is fair, just, loving and compassionate. This person is Kingdom directed and focused and is more concerned with caring for others than providing for himself or herself.

This person knows the Kingdom perspective of obedience because their *Identity* is established, and it is consistent. Everything to establish and secure your *Identity* in Christ is based upon the basic biblical principal of obedience. The easiest direction toward the most powerful understanding of obedience is to read and digest completely Proverbs 1:33. Here it reads

*"...WHOEVER LISTENS TO ME will dwell safely,*

*and will be secure, without fear of evil."*

First let's start with the obvious word "whoever"! This is simple yet powerful. Here we are to understand that this is an open invitation to all for a very specific reason, for a very specific Kingdom promise. We can read that even here, just like we learned in Psalm 37:23, God is directing your steps. Again, be reassured that your perfection is not the target of God. Your obedience and continuing progress are His concern.

Second that "listening" is of major importance to the completion of the promise. We started with a choice and even here, choice remains. I must not only choose to have God in my life, but I must also choose to listen. These are two essential core elements in securing our *Identity* and it may sound easier than it actually is. You see, in order for me to listen I must be silent. If I am going to listen to God, then I must come to the realization that my words are not as important as His. This obstacle is pride or self-righteousness.

The world is filled with this spirit as it has been there from the beginning. This spirit directly battles and opposes your *Identity*. If it can keep you from looking upon the Throne of God, then your understanding of who you are in the Kingdom of God will suffer and growth will not be present. Choosing correctly is a powerful position both in the natural and spiritual realms. I call this the beginning of the great establishment. I will explain further.

But let's get one thing perfectly stated and understood. Jesus conquered the enemy so that you could stand in victory. This victory is eternal and cannot be minimized nor erased. Your Identity in Christ is a powerful tool in the maintenance of peace in your life as well as the establishment of divine vision in completing what God has called you to complete.

Let's now take a look to further our understanding of the victory over the enemy that you are in possession of in this time. It all starts with a position, a place of understanding that you stand upon and for this discussion we will call this a "Position of Victory". Ephesians 1:17-21 tells us the following:

*Ephesians 1:17-21 [I always pray] that the God of our Lord Jesus Christ, the Father of glory, may grant you a spirit of wisdom and of revelation [that gives you a deep and personal and intimate insight] into the true knowledge of Him [for we know the Father through the Son...*

We must be in possession of the Holy Spirit, the deliverer of wisdom and revelation so we can arrive at a place of deep and personal knowledge of Jesus. In other words, so that we would have an intimate understanding of the Son of God in our lives. This is the basis and foundation of our true *Identity*. So when the thief comes in to take what does not belong to it, we would be prepared, ready in all directions. God wants you to live a life of abundance, to excel and to flourish in everything He has prepared for you. Here in John 10:10 we are reminded:

*"The thief comes only in order to steal and kill and destroy. I came that they may have and enjoy life, and have it in abundance [to the full, till it overflows]."*

Now let's direct our attention to a few areas of understanding. Remember, the enemy will attempt to send diversions and try to instill a fear in your life that you are alone, forgotten and powerless all in an effort to steal your Identity, so we must be on alert.

First and very importantly know that the enemy has been disarmed and humiliated. The word "disarmed" in Colossians 2:15 below speaks of God stripping Satan of all his weapons. The resurrection plundered the adversary. When Jesus rose from the dead He set a precedent that would never be attained. Jesus disarmed the supernatural forces of evil, those operating in and around our lives. Because He triumphed you participate in the victory and your *Identity* is established.

*When He had disarmed the rulers and authorities*

*[those supernatural forces of evil operating against us],*

*He made a public example of them*

*[exhibiting them as captives in His triumphal procession],*

*having triumphed over them through the cross.*

A major weapon in the establishment of your *Identity* is understanding your "comprehensive authority". This was given to you at a great price so that your Kingdom assignment and appointment would be attained and completed. Do not be surprised by the trials and tribulations you might encounter, just know that your Identity in Christ is constantly under attack by a world that does not want you to win. Within your possession is everything you will need to be successful. Luke 10:18-19 reminds us:

*He said to them, "I watched Satan fall from heaven*

*like [a flash of] lightning. Listen carefully:*

*I have given you authority [that you now possess]
to tread on serpents and scorpions, and
[the ability to exercise authority] over all
the power of the enemy (Satan);
and nothing will [in any way] harm you.*

The greater your understanding of *Identity* the greater will be your security and success. Remember, the enemy was defeated by Jesus Christ, so the it has no strength nor power over your life. Yet there are times we must be reminded of this very fact. Philippians 4:13 reminds us that our efforts are special and are extremely purposed.

Even in the midst of chaos and calamity found in the world, you can do anything, with great success, that which God has called you to do. When you are doing what God has called you to do then victory and completion is a guarantee. Protect your Identity from the thief at any expense. Continue your search for His Truth and this will not only strengthen you but it will bring you peace.

*I can do all things [which He has called me to do] through
Him who strengthens and empowers me [to fulfill His
purpose—I am self-sufficient in Christ's sufficiency; I am
ready for anything and equal to anything through Him who
infuses me with inner strength and confident peace.]*

Another critical awareness is the "call to the watchman". Our Identity requires that we maintain a balanced and self-disciplined life. This can only be achieved through a relationship that included the Word of God. This relationship means that we must never be separated from the Word and this is part of our early warning system so the enemy will never be able to catch you sleeping.

When I am out of balance, meaning my focus is on the things of the world, then I am exposed and unprepared to defend myself from the attacks that ensue. 1 Peter 5:8 warns us to be sober, to be awake and alert, never sleeping and always prepared. In this powerful reminder we are being empowered with revelation. The thief never stops. Like a lion in its search for food, it will not stop until it feeds. So must it be the same with us in the protection of our Identity.

*Be sober [well balanced and self-disciplined], be alert and cautious at all times. That enemy of yours, the devil, prowls around like a roaring lion [fiercely hungry], seeking someone to devour*

Because you choose Him and because you have chosen to listen to Him as He directs your life, you have now positioned yourself to receive. When the rest of the world is in natural and spiritual lack, you would be in the position to receive. What does this entail? The rest of Proverbs 1:33 describes receiving a life of safety, security and without fear! This is an amazing and most powerful promise. As the world begins to fall apart from fear of the natural conditions, you would be peaceful and unmoved because you are in possession of a powerful revelation. Your *Identity* is the key to this type of life, the type of life God has always wanted you to live. Not your life for yourself but His life for you! His plan for you!

This is your goal. Everyday make it your goal to *assess* and *reestablish* your Kingdom *Identity*. This may be a little uncomfortable as we might not be in the right place, but that's ok, do not let this deter you or discourage you. Just know that God continues to have an amazing and important plan for your life!

## PERSPECTIVES

### 1. God has a plan for you

*Regardless of where you are spiritually or what you have done in your past, the purpose of God for you has not and will not change. He loves you with an everlasting love which can never be exhausted nor redirected.*

### 2. Let God be God

*Rather than secure our own lives, let God be God. Trust in Him and He will manifest in your life. Your faith is what pleases and moves the Father. Trust, rely and adhere are all components to successful Faith. When these are present then doubt cannot be found in your life.*

### 3. A powerful source to manifestation: obedience

*When you are obedient then self in non-existent. It is easy to please self and ignore the Kingdom perspective. Obedience requires one to listen. Without listening to God then knowing His desires and His plan for your life becomes a weary burdened journey. His plan for you is to live a victorious life.*

Chapter 5

## IDENTITY is NEW

Like everything in our lives choice plays a critical role in our understanding, in our successes and even in our failures. How many times will I bump my head entering a low structure before I change the pattern. How many times will I continue to make the same mistakes, suffering the same outcome before I change my patterns?

We are a people of traditions and patterns. It seems that we find exceptional comfort and even security when we perform the same thing over and over. I am sure we can all recall some repeated exercise when the Christmas holidays make their rounds. Things we did as a child seem to find their way into our present. Stockings over the fireplace or door jam all in the same order, year after year. I am equally sure that if you were ever asked "why" you did this, your answer invariably would be "tradition".

While traditions in some things can be enjoyable they can also poison or prove themselves to be like weights or burdens especially when God is trying to do something new in our lives. When you have a solid understanding of who you are, your *Identity*, you will begin to envision the plan of God for you. We are reminded in Scripture many times to depart from our old ways and to embrace new ways and directions. Why? God is trying to rid us from error. Yes, we do learn hopefully from our mistakes but imagine living a life whereby mistakes could be avoided simply because you refused to perceive the old ways as possessing any value.

For many, departing from their old ways is a constant battle. Even when the struggles and problems encountered in the present all stem from roots of the past, habits and traditions are passed over. In 2 Corinthians 5:17 we are admonished and encouraged to change not only our understanding but our perspective too.

> "Therefore, if anyone is in Christ, he is a new creation;
> Old things have passed away; behold,
> all things have become new."

We are encouraged to see ourselves as "new". It is always exciting when we are in the presence of new. Whether it is a newly constructed home or the amazing smell of a new, never driven before, automobile, it is exciting. The reason for the excitement is that it represents a new start, a new opportunity for the future.

Before you accepted Jesus as your personal Savior life could be perceived as lifeless or even flatlined. Hope was elusive, and sadness or heaviness always filled the air you were breathing. Yet we are encouraged to see a position, a place to stand upon, that has always been there it was just that from our previous position it was near to impossible to see it. Jesus changed all of that for you!

A life of victory and success does not come from our old identification with the world. Jesus is calling us to see something different. Because of your hearts willingness to accept Him, change is the new catalyst, not our flesh. Reordering and reconstruction are now the process with every breath all in the plan of creating something new. This "new creation" is completely foreign to the world system. It appears different and even speaks different. It most definitely lives life differently and yes, it loves completely different than before. When Jesus becomes your focus, your *Identity* with the world begins to fade and a new connection is birthed. This connection to the supernatural is powerful and peaceful all at the same time.

This life of a newly understood *Identity* in Christ is only possible through the revelation of the Holy Spirit. I will discuss this further in another project, but the Presence of the Spirit of Jesus is invaluable and critical in forward movement and in the protection of your new *Identity*. Remember, when you accepted Jesus you became a new creation the likes of which the world has never seen before. So, it's no wonder that it may make attempts to strike back at you in various ways. Just remember that you are victorious now from where you stand spiritually. You are new! Your *Identity* is new!

In this new found or newly understood *Identity* it does come with some User Instructions. Usually we can refer to the ultimate of handbooks, The Bible, but here it is made simpler for you in 2 Corinthians 5:17 *"...old things have passed away..."*. This is amazing! No actually this is astounding! Everything about your old self and old ways.

The habits and traditions and even bad understandings have now passed. In other words, there is no value in these things. We are reminded that our new *Identity*, so precious and pure in the sight of God because of the sacrifice of Jesus, cannot be impacted by the past nor can it be weighed down by the past. You are highly favored in the eyes of your heavenly Father!

Yet we struggle with our old self. I know many who will read this have fought severe and continuing battles with their old selves. The spirit of condemnation comes in the late of the night or in the voices of those around you, reminding you of your past mistakes or of your failures. But I am here to shout and to blow the trumpet to sound an alarm. The darkness in this world will use any tool it can to take you back to that place in the past where you were once surrounded by confusion and the very darkness of ignorance. I encourage you to fight back in the spiritual realm with every weapon in your possession. Do not let it take your *Identity* nor let it deposit lies and deception into your ever-strengthening foundation.

*"All things have become new."* Did you hear what this verse is speaking into your spirit this very moment? The still small voice of God is speaking to you now! You have become new! This is not a suggestion nor is it an option. This is a statement, a command. It is reminding you that what once was is no longer and to make matters even more powerful, its very composition has changed. The original makeup of the subject has been reversed as it were, to its original condition. Imagine that! You were once old and now you have been made new. In the face of

a world that denounces anything that it cannot label nor explain, you have been taken to a new place. Everyone else will struggle with this supernatural journey of restoration.

## Passion and Authority

This is a powerful and divine position. Your *Identity* is in Jesus and will always remain in that place. No one will be able to remove you from that place unless you permit them to do so. You are always in control of the security of your *Identity*! Securing this newly found and understood asset is not as difficult as one would think. It does not require fancy theologies nor complicated doctrines. It does not need religiosity to be protected. But what it does depend on is your desire to do so. In other words, the protection of your *Identity* is solely dependent upon your desire and passion for the Will of God. You are a mighty, unfinished work and a highly prized possession of God. Ephesians 2:10 (AMP) tells us

*"For we are His workmanship [His own master work,*

*a work of art], created in Christ Jesus*

*[reborn from above—spiritually transformed, renewed,*

*ready to be used] for good works, which God prepared*

*[for us] beforehand [taking paths which He set],*

*so that we would walk in them [living the good life which*

*He prearranged and made ready for us]."*

Your very person was fashioned by the Most High God with a definite and perfect plan. Sure, at times things may not go according to plan. Yes, obstacles do sometimes find their way on the path that we travel. Do we stop our motion forward? Is the plan of God thwarted? To those who understand their *Identity* the answer to these two questions is a resounding "no". When the passion and zeal exist within us to seek the things of the Kingdom of God, when we learn that sometimes we must go over or through the obstacles because we know who we are, and we know the plan of God for us is to be victorious, then that is exactly what we do. Luke 10:19 (AMP) reminds you that your *Identity* in Christ comes with all of the necessary authority to get the job done

*"Listen carefully: I have given you authority [that you now possess] to tread on [a]serpents and scorpions, and [the ability to exercise authority] over all the power of the enemy (Satan); and nothing will [in any way] harm you."*

It's no wonder the plans of darkness are to cause you to be confused as to your Kingdom position. You are equipped to complete the work of God here on earth and He has ensured that you are in possession of every authority to do so with victory as the end result.

We are reminded daily through the Word of God that every day is an opportunity to show the Glory of God. You are a *"new creation"* and your old ways have passed away and everything before you in these hours are new because God has decreed that a perfect victory for you. What an exciting time in your life! What an amazing path you are traveling upon in these days. Do not let the plans of the enemy deter you from the ordained path set forth by God. Be reminded daily through His Word that His Grace and Mercy upon your life is endless and cannot be exhausted. Hebrews 4:16 (AMP) tells us

*"Therefore let us [with privilege] approach the throne of grace [that is, the throne of God's gracious favor] with confidence and without fear, so that we may receive mercy [for our failures] and find [His amazing] grace to help in time of need [an appropriate blessing, coming just at the right moment]."*

## A New Way of Thinking

You are a new creation and now must operate as such. The world does not have a grasp on you any longer, you are free. You are reminded daily to put on a new way of thinking. 2 Timothy 2:7 is a powerful weapon against spiritual ignorance which by the way is what we all fight on a daily basis. Your Identity in Christ is connected to a "New Way of Thinking".

More often than not when we are in a last ditch effort to win a race for an answer or solution, even to solve a situation, when we are in a place of desperation. It is here that the thief thrives, it is here that it is trying to weaken you and take from you. But God wants you to think over what he has said to you and about you. In this new way of thinking you will find reassurance and the strength that goes along with it. What does God have to say about this?

*"Think over the things I am saying*

*[grasp their application],*

*for the Lord will grant you*

<u>*insight and understanding*</u> *in everything."*

This is a powerful revelation for you. "Think over..." what God has spoken to you. He builds up your Identity. He strengthens your understanding of your Identity. This is all for His purpose and for His glory. He wants you to be Kingdom Inspired and to possess Kingdom Insight for an increased understanding of your assignment that He has appointed you to complete. Let's revisit a life altering Scripture 2 Corinthians 5:17...

*"Therefore, if anyone is in Christ, he is a new creation;*

*old things have passed away; behold,*

*all things have become new."*

In this new season of your life there are some requirements, there will be some resources you will have to expend. First your Identity will require that you be "teachable" and secondly you will need to be "leadable". These are not subject to our decisions nor arguments, these are set in stone and require each other to solidfy a powerful foundation. This is a powerful revelation.

Now that you are in a new season of revelation of your Identity, there are some co-laboring efforts needed. First you must reject conformity, reject the desire wanting to be like the rest or to simply fit in. The Kingdom of God demands that we not be like the world. The rejection of conformity is confirmed in Romans 12:2 we again are reminded:

*And do not be conformed to this world [any longer with its superficial values and customs], but*
*be transformed and progressively changed [as you mature spiritually] by the renewing of your mind [focusing on godly values and ethical attitudes], so that you may prove [for yourselves] what the will of God is,*
*that which is good and acceptable and perfect [in His plan and purpose for you].*

When we are separated from that which is not from God then we conform to that which encircles us. So it stands as a divine truth, do not conform yourselves to what is separating you from. Why? Your Identity is important to God and to His purpose in you that must be fulfilled. Be on alert!

> *1 Pet 1:13-16 …. not conforming yourselves to the former lusts, as in your ignorance….*

It is important that we understand not through the lens of religion but through the divine truth of His promises to us. Because of the Blood of Jesus, because of this ultimate and precious sacrifice, yes, it is a privilege to be able to approach the Throne of God. Before your *Identity* was changed, before you accepted Jesus as your personal Savior, it was impossible to come into the Holy of Holies. But because of this sacrifice and shedding of Blood, you and I can enter into this place with the full understanding and assurance that all of my failures and errors are forgiven, and mercy takes their place. Yes, in those desperate hours of failure or condemnation, when escape routes are not visible, there is a way in the desert that has been carved just for you!

> *Behold, I will do a new thing, now it shall spring forth; shall you not know it? I will even make a road in the wilderness and rivers in the desert. (Isaiah 43:19)*

Chapter 6

# 5 EQUIPPINGS TO PROTECT and GUARD YOUR IDENTITY

The first equipping is to *Set Your Mind on Things Above*. There is a place that you must stand upon to be secure. The foundation is to be deep and trusted. To protect and guard your *Identity* successfully then you will need to be trained and then you will need to employ what you have learned. Like any well-trained soldier, training is critical, but a time will come whereby you must use what you have been given.

The bible teaches us in Colossians 3:2 to

*"Set your mind on things above,
not on things on the earth."*

Your security and your protection come from a place of Divine origin. God, through the Blood of Jesus, has instructed us to take great aim, a great focus. Rather than do as the world would have you do, to focus on your day to day fleshly requirements, make your focus on heavenly things. In other words, arrest and halt every thought that does not have a God oriented purpose.

This is not easy because we are bombarded constantly with dark and sometimes evil thoughts, but this is the battle and He has assured us that we have won this fight. You are victorious in this battle!

To protect what God has given you, know that your security comes from your focus on Him, His plan for you and even His support for you. He leads us toward valuable and critical wisdom. Your thoughts are to be selective, sifted and highly focused toward Him. Toward heavenly and Divine things! Disregard the hateful and hurtful words and actions from those around you. Do not focus on the broken promises of a weakened humanity. When you are focused on the purpose and plan of God for you, then your *Identity* cannot be stolen nor compromised.

The second equipping is to *Possess the Mind of Christ*. Very similar in direction and importance to the above is found in 1 Corinthians 2:16

*"...who has known the mind of the Lord that he may instruct Him?" But we have the mind of Christ."*

Truly what is the "mind of Christ"? It may seem that it would be unattainable for us, yet this is a directive that comes from God Himself. We are to live with the possession of the mind of Christ, which can be defined as that very focus that Jesus was in possession of, the Fathers Will.

When we are in possession knowing the Father's Will for us, then we are in possession of the mind of Christ. One cannot attain such wisdom or knowledge without, first the presence of the Holy Spirit and secondly, being so close to the Father as to understand and know His Will.

Jesus knew the Father's Will and Plan at all times. When your relationship is so passionate and zealous for the things of God, your relationship with Him becomes your daily driving force. Your possession of the mind of Christ not only secures your *Identity* but it also gives you the strength needed to survive your life's storms.

The third equipping is to *Not Engage the Contrary in Conversation*. How many times have we tried to have the last word in a discussion or even an argument. It seems that speaking the last word in such an encounter would be the equivalent to some distorted victory of sorts. When we attempt to speak and make our position known to what appears to be the obstinate or ignorant may very well be a spiritual trap set to slowly dismantle the walls surrounding your *Identity*.

Sometimes we just need to be silent during the war because not all wars are the same. 2 Corinthians 10:3-4 teaches us:

*"For though we walk in the flesh, we do not war according to the flesh. For the weapons of our warfare are not carnal but mighty in God for pulling down strongholds..."*

Your *Identity* must be protected from speaking or reacting to the enemy because you might be bated into saying something that you might regret. Never lose sight that the battle you might be fighting is a spiritual battle and not just a battle in the flesh. Your *Identity* as a son and or daughter of God is visible in the darkness. We are warned that attack will come. Persecution for His Namesake will come. If we set our mind on divine things and remain in possession with the Mind of Christ on both the natural and spiritual battlefields, your *Identity* will be secure!

The fourth equipping in securing and protecting your Identity is to *Take Every Thought Captive*. This may seem simplistic but in reality, it can be difficult if one does not practice.

We live in a fallen world, saturated with darkness, evil and perversions. All of these are aimed to disrupt and even destroy what God is doing in your life making it impossible to hear Him. As we see in the first 3 Equipping's, your mind is the target and it must be protected. If you think like the world then your understanding of who you are in Christ, your *Identity*, will diminish. You are to take every measure available to you to protect yourself. We read in 2 Corinthians 10:5 our military orders:

*"...casting down arguments and every high thing that exalts itself against the knowledge of God, bringing every thought into captivity to the obedience of Christ..."*

Here they are, your Divine Orders! Everything that comes your way that does not align itself with the Word of God in your life, is an argument against God Himself. Cast it down. Just like a fisherman casting a line out at sea, cast the line far away from the boat. Get as much distance between you and the liar as possible. This in effect is like imprisoning the evil and keeping it away from you.

If you find yourself depressed or heavy with condemnation, it is because you have not cast the liar away from your camp. God has called you to a victorious life but if you listen to the defeating remarks of the enemy, if you continue to surround yourself with arguments that oppose the plans of God for you and in your life, then do not be surprised any longer, your *Identity* is at risk!

You were created to be in control at all times. In fact God reassured you that He would be handing you Kingdom Authority to get the job done. Start today to cast any statement spoken to you by man or even religion that does not align itself with God's plan over your life.

Protect your *Identity* and start casting and removing from your life, words that directly argue with God. Secure your mind with His Word and know that nothing can separate you from the love of God!

The final and very critical equipping is to *Keep His Words in Your Mouth*. A day without the Word of God to focus upon is like a day without your morning coffee or tea or even better yet, it is like a day without oxygen. In other words, you will not get too far before you pass out and fall.

In Deuteronomy 30:14 you are encouraged to not only establish a closeness with the Word of God but to also understand that it is a catalyst to Divine movement. It reads:

*"But the word is very near you, in your mouth and in your heart, that you may do it."*

One of the most common and sometimes effective ploys of the enemy is to keep you silent. When you do not speak then you are not speaking of the Kingdom nor the plans of God for you. In this example, people who cross your path, those who God has orchestrated to intersect your line of travel, will never be affected by His Word. You see, the Word of God in your mouth and upon your tongue must be heard by the world. The plan of the opposition is to keep you silent so that none of it is ever heard!

To make matters even more complicated, when we do not speak what God has poured into us we too will not receive the maximum benefit and plan of God for our lives. If you notice the last portion of the aforementioned Scripture states that there is a place where the Word of God resides within you. The two places mentioned are your mouth and your heart. Remember what we are taught through Luke 6:45:

*"A good man out of the good treasure of his heart brings forth good; and an evil man out of the evil treasure of his heart[a] brings forth evil. For out of the abundance of the heart his mouth speaks."*

So, it stands to reason that when my heart is full of evil and darkness that is exactly what it will express. But when it is filled to the brim with life and encouragement, that is what I will speak of and that is what I will live!

Let's return to Deuteronomy 30:14:

*"But the word is very near you, in your mouth and in your heart, that you may do it."*

It is obvious that through His Word to us God is asking us to be aware of the two components that are important to Him, your mouth and your heart. But He is also warning us to protect them as they are important to the expansion of His Kingdom on earth and to our spiritual *Identity*. Again, if you do not speak then how will anyone come to know the power of God operating in your life? In fact everything about your relationship with God and everything about your spiritual growth points to the last portion of verse 14. You must take what you have and cause it to be set in motion or in other words "that you may do it".

When the opposition takes the authority in your life then you will become silent and what God is speaking through you will never be heard by a dark and dying world. Your *Identity* is priceless to the Kingdom of God so protecting it is a full-time activity. Again, what God has given you must be released to those around you. In return He will ensure more is given to you!

When you begin to feel the presence of the opposition or when things in life begin to present themselves as out of order, come back to this short reminder. Protecting your *Identity* from theft by the enemy is easier than you think. You will not need special tools, nor will you need to expend thousands of dollars. Yes, there will be an investment that will be required but it is purely in desire. Your *Identity* must be protected at all costs!

So, let's recap the 5 Equipping's to protect and guard your *Identity*:

## 1. Set Your Mind on Things Above

*Set your mind on things above, not on things on the earth. (Colossians 3:2)*

There is a very specific place your mind must rest upon. Chaos and confusion are not present when our minds are focused on God plans and directives.

## 2. Possess the Mind of Christ

*...who has known the mind of the Lord that he may instruct Him? But WE HAVE the mind of Christ. (1 Corinthians 2:16)*

The defeat of chaos and the confusion of the darkness are a completed promise for us. Yet God wants us to co-labor with Him in this process through possessing the mind of Christ. It is from that place we will know His complete peace and plans for our lives.

## 3. Not Engage the Contrary in Conversation

*For though we walk in the flesh, we do not war according to the flesh. For the weapons of our warfare are not carnal but mighty in God for pulling down strongholds... (1 Corinthians 10:3-4)*

Stay clear from conversations with the religious minded person and spirit. Those who refuse to leave behind their religiosity only desire to trap you in their confusion.

## 4. Take Every Thought Captive

*...casting down arguments and every high thing that exalts itself against the knowledge of God, bringing every thought into captivity to the obedience of Christ... (2 Corinthians 10:5)*

Take the thoughts from the enemy, arrest them and place them into captivity through the Word of God. You are always in control when you are in possession of your *Identity*.

## 5. Keep His Words in Your Mouth

*But the word is very near you, in your MOUTH and in your HEART, that you may do it. (Deuteronomy 30:14)*

The Word of God reminds us that when we draw near to the Father, He would draw near to us. So, when His Word is in My mouth and heart then I am closest to Him. The more I speak of Him, praise Him and exalt Him, the closer our relationship becomes. From this place, there is no room for the thief... your *Identity* is the safest from this place!

# A Life Without Limitations

*Phil 4:13 I can do all things [which He has called me to do] through Him who strengthens and empowers me [to fulfill His purpose—I am self-sufficient in Christ's sufficiency; I am ready for anything and equal to anything through Him who infuses me with inner strength and confident peace.]*

*(Philippians 4:13)*

God wants you to live a life without limits, in fact if we are limited in anything, chains and imprisonment might be present. Jesus defeated the enemy thus securing our rightful place in the presence of God the Father. It is time to break the chains of tradition and corporate religion. It is time to put the religious spirit on notice and declare that you too are a son and daughter of the Most High God!

Stay in the Presence of God through His Word and through the revelation of the Holy Spirit. Continue to protect your *Identity* as the thief is on the prowl to weaken and even destroy it.

Remember you serve a mighty God and there is nothing in the natural realm that can have any success in stopping you. God has chosen you!

There might be obstacles in your life at present but be blessed in the knowledge of God that He has authored an amazing and beautiful plan for your life. Your *Identity* is critical to His Work and the completion of it.

Chapter 7

# DEVOTIONS

## Prophetic Words of Divine Encouragement

**A LIFE OF CONFIDENCE**

*Romans 15:13 May the God of hope fill you with all joy & peace in believing [through the experience of your faith] that by the power of the Holy Spirit you will abound in hope and overflow with confidence in His promises...*

- Get excited about the gospel & your faith in Jesus

- Overflow with confidence in His promises

**SPIRITUAL DISCIPLINES: GODLINESS**

*1 Timothy 4:7 But have nothing to do with irreverent folklore and silly myths. On the other hand, discipline yourself for the purpose of godliness [keeping yourself spiritually fit].*

- Let God correct you through the Holy Spirit. He will always direct you towards growth.

## FAITH BUILDING BLOCKS

### FEED

*Psalm 34:8 O taste and see that the Lord [our God] is good; How blessed [fortunate, prosperous, and favored by God] is the man who takes refuge in Him....*

### EXERCISE

*James 2:17 .....faith, if it does not have works [to back it up], is by itself dead [inoperative and ineffective].*

### SPEAK

*2 Corinthians 4:13 ....we have the same spirit of faith as he had, who wrote in Scripture, "I believed, therefore I spoke." We also believe, therefore we also speak....*

### STAY PUT

*Heb 10:38-39 But My righteous one [the one justified by faith] shall live by faith [respecting man's relationship to God and trusting Him]; and if he draws back [shrinking in fear], My soul has no delight in him.*

### RESISTANCE

*James 4:7 So submit to [the authority of] God. <u>RESIST</u> the devil [stand firm against him] and he will flee from you.*

## LISTEN

Isa 41:13 For I the Lord your God keep hold of your right hand; [I am the Lord], <u>WHO SAYS TO YOU</u>, 'Do not fear, I will help you.'

## PRAISE GOD IN YOUR LIFE

### 1. PRAISE God

Psalm 150:2 Praise Him for His mighty acts; Praise Him according to [the abundance of] His greatness.

### 2. PRAISE and APPROACH

Psalm 95:2-3 Let us come before His presence with a song of thanksgiving; Let us shout joyfully to Him with songs.

### 3. PRAISE will DEFEAT the ADVERSARY

2 Chronicles 20:22 When they began SINGING and PRAISING, the Lord set ambushes against the sons of Ammon, Moab, and Mount Seir, who had come against Judah; so they were STRUCK DOWN [in defeat].

### 4. PRAISE INCREASES our FOCUS on GOD

Ps 103:2-4 Bless and affectionately praise the Lord, O my soul, and do not forget any of His benefits; who forgives all your sins, who heals all your diseases; who redeems your life from the pit, who crowns you [lavishly] with lovingkindness and tender mercy;

### 5. PRAISE is the FRUIT of LIPS

Hebrews 13:15 Through Him, therefore, let us at all times offer up to God a SACRIFICE OF PRAISE, which is the fruit of lips that thankfully acknowledge & confess & GLORIFY HIS NAME.


## FLOURISH and to EXCEL

Job 8:7 Though your beginning was INSIGNIFICANT.....your END will GREATLY INCREASE.
- God is with you even in the meager beginnings
- There is divine increase when you continue


## DESTINED to be EFFECTIVE

Philippians 2:13 For it is [not your strength, but it is] God who is EFFECTIVELY AT WORK IN YOU, both to will and to work [that is, strengthening, energizing, and creating in you the longing and the ability to fulfill your purpose] for His good pleasure.

- God is at work in you for an effective life
- These represent the purpose of God

## WAITING

*Philippians 1:6 ….. He who has begun a good work in you will perfect and complete it*

- Be confident that what God started will be finished!

## VICTORY

*Ephesians 2:10 …..we are His workmanship for good works, which God prepared beforehand…..*

- You are destined to Walk in victory!

## COMPLETION

*Psalm 138:8 The Lord will accomplish that which concerns me…..*

- Completion concerns the Will of God for you.

## PURPOSE

*Obadiah 1:1 ….Thus says the Lord God concerning Edom we have heard a report from the Lord, & a Messenger (ambassador) has been sent among the nations, saying, "Arise, & let us rise up against her for battle...*

## ABOUT THE AUTHOR

Apostle Dr. Ric Perez is a longtime resident of California. He and his wife Pastor Maria, who also co-serves as Senior Pastor of ATtheWELL, have been married for 37 years.

Ric was raised a Catholic and encountered the true and living Christ years ago, was baptized in the Name of Jesus and filled with the Holy Spirit. He was ordained as Pastor by Rod Parsley and soon after ordained as Prophet. Both Dr. Ric and Pastor Maria have a passion to break the walls of religion and tradition across the world.

Apostle Ric has attended several universities in furthering his education with a degree in Criminal Justice which assisted him in bringing the Word of God into the prisons. Through this Kingdom effort many thousands have received Jesus as their personal Savior while several thousand have been immersed in the waters of Baptism. He has completed his Masters in Theology and has received his Doctorate in Theology.

Dr. Ric and Pastor Maria have followed the direction of the Holy Spirit, ministering and planting several churches across California, they have developed a powerful presence in social media with over 50,000 followers all to glorify God.

Because of their love for God, ATtheWELL has been taken to a global status with thousands across the world hearing the prophetic teachings and empowering Word of the Holy Spirit.